ANCIENT CIVILIZATIONS

Mesopotamia

By Tami Deedrick

Raintree Steck-Vaughn Publishers

A Harcourt Company

Austin · New York
www.steck-vaughn.com

Published by Raintree Steck-Vaughn Publishers,
an imprint of Steck-Vaughn Company.

Library of Congress Cataloging-in-Publication Data
    Mesopotamia/by Tami Deedrick.
        p.cm.—(Ancient civilizations)
    Includes bibliographical references and index.
    ISBN 0-7398-3584-X
    1. Iraq—Civilization—To 634—Juvenile literature. [1. Iraq—Civilization—
To 634.] I. Title. II. Ancient civilizations (Raintree Steck-Vaughn)
DS71 .D43 2001
935—dc21

                                            2001019860

Printed and bound in the United States of America
1 2 3 4 5 6 7 8 9 10 WZ 05 04 03 02 01

Produced by Compass Books

Photo Acknowledgments
Corbis/Roger Wood, cover; Dean Conger, title page; Gianni Dagli Orti, 6, 10,
14, 16, 19, 20, 25,
   26, 29, 32, 36; David Lees, 9; Charles Lenars, 22; Bettmann, 30;
   Diego Lezama Orezzoli, 34; Francoise de Mulder, 43

Content Consultants
Christopher Rose
Outreach Coordinator
Center for Middle Eastern Studies
The University of Texas at Austin

Don L. Curry
Educational Author, Editor, Consultant, and Columnist

Contents

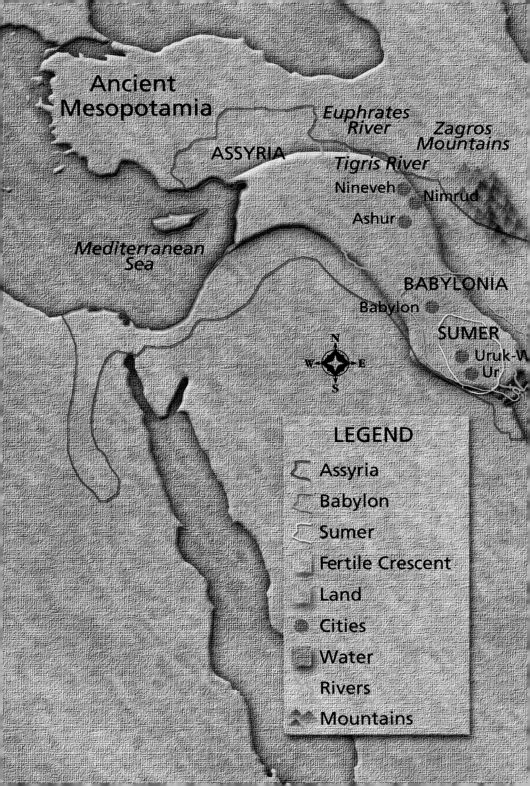

Mesopotamian History

Mesopotamia was one of the world's oldest civilizations. In a civilization, people are part of an advanced **society** and share a way of life. People settled in villages and began to grow plants and raise animals in about 9000 B.C. In about 3500 B.C., Mesopotamians first began living together in cities. Before this time, there were no cities.

Mesopotamia means "the land between the rivers." It was between the Tigris and Euphrates Rivers in the Middle East. This strip of land was also called the Fertile Crescent because it had water and good soil. Because of this, Mesopotamians could grow enough food to feed large numbers of people.

▲ This carving shows the kings of two
city-states greeting each other.

City-States

Mesopotamia was made up of about
20 city-states. A city-state is a tiny nation
built around a central town. After 2300 B.C.
people in Mesopotamia formed the first
central government ruled by a king.

Every city-state had its own king and
army. The king controlled and made rules for

the city-state. The people of each city often had a favorite god or goddess to worship. To worship is to serve the gods. They built **temples** for their chosen gods. A temple is a special building for worshiping and serving the gods.

Life was different in each city-state. Each city had its own rules and favorite gods. Still, all Mesopotamians had things in common. They dressed alike and believed in gods and goddesses. Their homes and temples were built the same. People visited other city-states to buy and sell goods.

For much of Mesopotamian history, city-states never joined into one country. In fact, they were almost always fighting wars with each other. They fought to get more land or to control the water supply.

Sometimes one city-state became more powerful than others. Its army would capture other city-states and make them give tribute, or payments. The ruling city-state would also take people back to their city as slaves. A slave is someone owned by someone else.

Inside a City-State

Most city-states were home to 50,000 to 100,000 people. Cities often had tall walls around them. The walls helped keep them safe from enemy armies. Farm fields and small villages surrounded the city. If there was a war, people moved inside the city walls.

Sometimes large ziggurats were built in the center of city-states. A ziggurat was a building with many levels, called platforms. Each platform was a little smaller than the one on the bottom. This made the building look like a mountain with a flat top. Stairs connected the levels. A temple was at the very top of the ziggurat.

A walled area called the temple complex surrounded some ziggurats. Many buildings were located in the temple complex, including a large palace, or home for the king. Courts, buildings for storing food, schools that taught writing, and homes for **priests** and priestesses were also there. These men and women worked in temples and

▲ This picture shows a ziggurat and the remains of an ancient city-state's walls.

served the gods. At times, large open markets also surrounded the temple.

People built their houses outside the temple-complex walls. They lived along thin, winding roads. The houses were close together. People from nearby villages traveled to the city to buy and trade goods. Some stayed inside the city walls if there was a war.

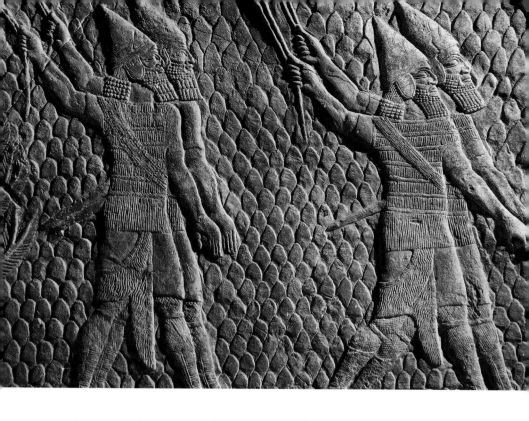

This carving shows Mesopotamian soldiers fighting with slingshots.

Early Mesopotamian History

The rule of Mesopotamia often changed throughout history. Many groups of people lived there. Each group built their own city-states and fought each other for power.

The Sumerians controlled southern Mesopotamia from about 2800 to 2350 B.C.

Their major city-states were Uruk-Warka, Kish, and Lagash. Sumerians dug waterways called canals to irrigate the soil. To irrigate is to pipe or carry water to dry land. Because of this, farmers were able to grow enough food for many people. This made it possible for civilization to begin.

From about 2350 to 2190 B.C., Akkadian kings united and ruled Mesopotamia. They originally lived in northern Mesopotamia. Their major city-state was Akkad. An Akkadian king named Sargon went to war and united many of the city-states in the north and south. By doing this, Sargon formed the first **empire** of the world. An empire is a group of countries that all have the same ruler.

After the Akkadian kings, Sumerian kings took over their empire again for a brief time. Then, the first Assyrian Empire conquered northern Mesopotamia. They were conquered by a king named Hammurabi.

MESOPOTAMIA TIMELINE

4500 B.C.	Sumerians begin to live together in cities.
4000 B.C.	Sumerians start using wheeled vehicles.
3100 B.C.	Cuneiform begins to develop.
2650 B.C.	Gilgamesh is king of Uruk.
2350 B.C.	Akkadian king Sargon captures and unites cities.
2170 B.C.	Sumer regains control of Mesopotamia.
2100 B.C.	Ur-Nammu rules and builds the first ziggurat.
1900 B.C.	Amorites build Babylon.
1792 B.C. to 1750 B.C.	Hammurabi is king of Babylon.
1595 B.C.	Kassites control Babylon.
900 B.C.	Assyrians take control and make Nineveh their capital.
612 B.C.	Chaldeans capture Nineveh and Babylon rules again.
604 B.C. to 562 B.C.	Nebuchadnezzar II builds Hanging Gardens of Babylon.
539 B.C.	Cyrus of Persia captures Babylon.

Later Mesopotamian History

The Amorites ruled Mesopotamia from about 1900 to 1600 B.C. Their main city-state was Babylon. Because of this, the Amorites became known as the Babylonians. Their best-known king was Hammurabi. His court decisions were written on stones like laws.

For several hundred years, many different groups fought each other for power. At about 900 B.C., the Assyrians from north of Babylon gained control of Mesopotamia again. Nineveh was one of their capitals. The Assyrians destroyed many other city-states and brought people back to Nineveh as slaves. The Assyrians also built roads for their armies.

A group of people called the Chaldeans took over Mesopotamia in 612 B.C. The Chaldeans were also known as the neo-Babylonians. Neo means new. They made Babylon their capital.

In 539 B.C., the Persians went to war with Mesopotamians. They captured Babylon and made Mesopotamia part of the Persian Empire.

This statue is of an ancient king of Mesopotamia.

Daily Life of the Mesopotamians

There were different groups of people in Mesopotamian society. People were part of a group depending on their land, money, or family. In Mesopotamia, people could join a higher group in society. But most people stayed in the same group throughout their lives.

The king and his family were the richest and most powerful. They lived in large palaces and had many servants. They controlled many farms.

Army officers and government workers were often rich and powerful, too. Judges and scribes were some of these government workers. Unlike most Mesopotamians, scribes were men who could read and write.

▲ This carving shows Mesopotamian working-class men carrying offerings.

Other People in Mesopotamian Society

Craftspeople and merchants were not as wealthy or powerful. Craftspeople made goods, such as cloth, tools, and art. Merchants were people who bought, sold, and traded goods.

Farmers and shepherds made up another group. Shepherds raise and care for animals.

Slaves were also present. They were usually prisoners of war. Sometimes slaves were people who owed money and who had to work off their debt, usually for up to seven years. There were also large numbers of people who did not own their farms and worked for the king or other landowners.

Clothing

Mesopotamians made clothes out of wool or thread-like flax fibers. Flax is a plant.

During the summer, Mesopotamians wore loose clothes made of flax. During cool winter weather, the people wore animal skins or heavier clothes made from wool.

Men wrapped a long piece of cloth around their waist and tied it in front. Instead of shirts, men sometimes wore long shawls. They tied their shawls over one shoulder and left the other bare.

Women wore long dresses. Dresses often draped across the left shoulder, and the right shoulder was bare. In cool weather, women wore shawls over both shoulders.

Hair and Jewelry

Women had long hair. They often braided their hair and wrapped it around their heads. Sometimes they tied their hair into a knot that hung down their backs.

Mesopotamians wore different kinds of head coverings. Some noble women wore headdresses decorated with flowers and leaves. Some kings wore a tall, gold headpiece as a crown. Kings in the third and fourth centuries wore cloth caps. Both men and women wore a lot of jewelry, such as necklaces, bracelets, and earrings.

Country Homes

Mesopotamians built homes out of the materials available on their land. There was not much wood or stone. People had to trade goods with other countries to get these materials. Usually, only homes of the rich had any wood or stone inside them.

The first Mesopotamians made their houses out of reeds. These huts were small and round. They had no windows.

> This mask shows a Mesopotamian woman wearing a headdress.

By 4,000 B.C., all Mesopotamians made bricks out of mud, clay, and straw because these lasted longer than reeds. The bricks were dried in the sun until they were hard. Builders used soft mud to stick the bricks together. They used a tar called **bitumen** to stick stones together.

These are the remains of King Nebuchadnezzar's palace.

 The Hanging Gardens of Babylon are one of the Seven Wonders of the Ancient World. Nebuchadnezzar II built the gardens for his wife Amyitis. She was from Mede, a place with mountains, trees, and green plants. In Babylon, there was not enough rain for these things to grow on the flat, dusty land. Nebuchadnezzar had workers build a mountain of terraces. They planted trees, flowers, and green plants on the terraces.

City Homes

In southern cities, Mesopotamians built square houses around open courtyards. Thick, windowless walls, low doorways, and trees in the courtyards helped keep the houses cool.

Some people built houses with two levels. The family lived on the upper floor while any slaves or visitors used the lower floor. Roofs were flat. People often slept on the roofs during hot weather.

Some people believe Mesopotamian homes did not have much furniture. Instead, they usually sat on pillows or rugs instead of chairs.

These are the remains of a Mesopotamian ziggurat that was built for the gods.

Mesopotamian Culture

The way of life, ideas, and traditions of a group of people make up their **culture**. The Mesopotamians expressed their culture in the things they made.

Religion was the center of Mesopotamian culture. People believed that they were servants of the gods. Mesopotamians honored their gods by giving offerings or by building huge temples. In this way, they felt they were serving the gods.

Many Mesopotamian pictures and statues are of their gods. Their largest buildings were usually temples or ziggurats. To honor their gods, Mesopotamians held religious gatherings filled with dancing and singing.

Architecture

Architecture is the style and way a building is made. Mesopotamians built their best works of architecture for their gods. They built many temples.

Mesopotamians began building ziggurats in the third century B.C. To do this, people leveled the temples when they started to fall apart or get old. This formed a platform. Then, they built another temple on top of the new platform. They repeated this process until some temples sat on top of seven platforms. Together, all the platforms formed a pyramid-like ziggurat.

Ziggurats reached high into the sky toward the gods. Often people had to walk through large, arched gates to come near the ziggurat. On the top of the ziggurat, tall columns supported the roofs of the temples.

Mesopotamians were the first to invent the arch. They built an arch by fitting wedge-shaped bricks together to form a half-circle shape.

Rules

Without rules for behavior, civilization would not have begun. Kings in Mesopotamia set up the first set of rules. They also set up courts for those who did not follow the rules.

Some believe that King Hammurabi of Babylon wrote one of the first codes of law. He had 282 of his court decisions carved on four pillars of black stone. They stood 7 feet (210 cm) tall. He put the pillars in places where people could see them.

The decisions of Hammurabi were written on this black stone pillar.

▲ **Mesopotamian artists made this metal knife and its decorated holder.**

Art

Mesopotamians are known for their life-like statues. They are full of detail in their faces and clothing. Artists formed most statues and sculptures out of metals, such as gold, silver, and bronze.

In about 800 B.C., one common type of statue was a large beast with wings. This winged beast was a symbol of greatness and power. The beasts had human heads with bodies of lions or bulls. Huge wings attached to the backs of the statues.

Some of the most important statues were of the gods. A temple housed the statue of the god for whom it was built. Everyday the priests of the temple took care of the god. They gave the god a bath, put clothes on it, and offered it food.

Mesopotamians also used some stone and colored tiles to decorate the inside of temples and palaces. They carved pictures into the stone. Most of the pictures were of the gods or powerful kings who built the temples.

Colorful pictures called **mosaics** covered some ziggurat walls. Mesopotamian artists made the mosaics by sticking painted pegs into the soft clay walls. The pegs formed a pattern or picture in many bright colors.

Language and Writing

Mesopotamians invented the first form of writing. Scribes used a **stylus** to press pictures into soft clay. A stylus is a writing tool with a thick, square-shaped end and a thin end. To keep the clay moist, people covered the clay tablets with wet cloth until they were finished writing. After the writing was done, they left the clay in the sun to harden.

The earliest writing was **pictographs** scratched into clay. Mesopotamians used this writing to keep records of taxes, tributes, and things they owned. They used dots, half-moons, and thumbnail prints for numbers and pictures for items. An ox with three lines meant the person owned three oxen.

Mesopotamians then began combining pictures to make new meanings. A stick figure of a man next to an ox might mean a farmer. The pictures started looking less like pictures and more like a series of lines and wedges. This form of writing became known as cuneiform, which means "wedge-shaped" in Latin.

This clay tablet is covered with cuneiform writing.

Scribes were the only Mesopotamians who could read and write in cuneiform. It was hard to learn the language. Powerful people sent one of their sons to scribe school when they were six years old. They copied clay tablets from morning to night. They stayed in school until they were men.

▲ This clay seal shows a scene from the *Epic of Gilgamesh*.

Literature

Mesopotamians were the first people to write **epics**. An epic is a long story or poem about the adventures and battles of a king, god, or hero.

One of the most popular religious epics from Mesopotamia was the *Epic of Gilgamesh*. The real Gilgamesh was king of Uruk in 2700 B.C. The epic tells about Gilgamesh and his friend Enkidu. Together, they fought gods and monsters. One story tells how Gilgamesh and Enkidu killed a monster named Hambaba. Another tells of the two battling the Bull of Heaven and winning.

Mesopotamians also wrote down wise sayings called proverbs. Proverbs are people's ideas about life.

At Nineveh, **archaeologists** found a great library full of Mesopotamian literature. An archaeologist is a scientist who studies ruins to learn about the past. The library of clay tablets was started by the Assyrian king Ashurbanipal who ruled from 669 to 630 B.C. This was one of the first libraries in the world.

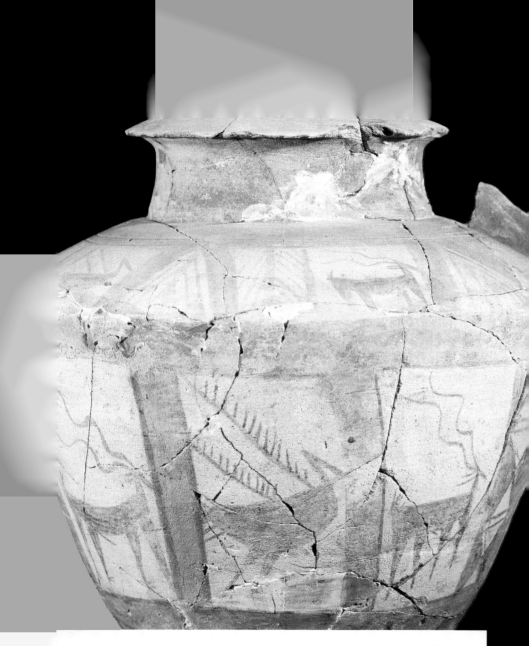

Mesopotamians decorated much of their pottery with animal pictures.

What Did the Mesopotamians Do?

The Mesopotamian civilization created advanced technology. Technology is the use of science and knowledge to make tools and produce products. With technology, people make new things to improve their lives.

Scientists believe the Mesopotamian people were also the first to farm, make glass, cloth and **pottery**, and form metal into objects. In fact, Mesopotamians were using a wheel to make pottery as early as 4000 B.C. Pottery is objects made out of clay.

The Mesopotamians starting using wheels to move things around. Wheels under a platform made it easier to move things. The Mesopotamians added sides to make carts.

 These are the remains of an ancient reservoir used for storing water.

Farming

Farming was important to the Mesopotamian way of life. Farmers grew wheat, barley, and vegetables. They grew fruit trees, such as date and pomegranate. Cucumbers, onions, and lettuce were popular vegetables.

Mesopotamians practiced shade gardening. They planted trees to shade the crops from the hot sun and strong winds.

Mesopotamians invented tools to help them farm. To help plant the seeds, farmers developed plows made out of bronze and iron. Farmers used animals to drag plows along the ground to break up the soil.

Another type of plow dug a furrow, or long thin row, for planting. It had a tube on it. A farmer walked next to the plow and dropped seeds through the tube. In this way, the seeds fell into the furrow.

Mesopotamians dug long canals from the Euphrates and Tigris Rivers to their dry fields. People captured and stored rainwater in reservoirs. These are holding places for water.

Mesopotamians also built aqueducts. An aqueduct is a pipe or channel built to carry water. Aqueducts brought water from mountain springs into cities. Without aqueducts, people in cities would not have had enough water.

▲ This carving shows Mesopotamian sailors transporting wood logs by boat.

Transportation

Transportation is a way of moving things. To move goods up and down the rivers, Mesopotamians needed to make boats. They tried many different materials and shapes to see what worked the best.

The raft worked well. The Mesopotamians built large platforms out of logs. Then they attached animal skins under the platforms. They filled the skins with air to make the raft float. At the end of the trip, they took the raft apart and sold the logs. The animal skins were small enough to take back on foot or by donkey.

Another boat was the coracle. Boat builders covered a light wood frame with animal skins. They covered the whole boat with bitumen to make it waterproof. This boat was light enough to carry on a person's shoulders. Mesopotamians invented sails on boats, which helped them travel farther and faster.

Mesopotamians also invented **chariots**. A chariot is a small vehicle pulled by an animal. It looks like a barrel with the back cut off. Mesopotamians used chariots mainly during war. A soldier stood on the chariot and steered the animal.

Math and Science

The Mesopotamians made huge advances in math and science. They developed a way of counting and a numbering system that still survives today. The Mesopotamians based their numbering system on the number 60. Their system also included numbers that could be evenly divided into 60, such as the number 12. Today's 60-second minute, 60-minute hour, and 12-hour clock come from the Mesopotamian system.

Mesopotamians were the first to start a system of weights and measurements. This allowed Mesopotamians to have a fair way to trade. They made the first standard lengths, such as a foot.

Some Mesopotamians became astronomers who studied the sky. The astronomers recorded the movements of the Sun and planets. They studied the stars and the Moon.

Other Mesopotamians became astrologers who looked for messages from the gods in

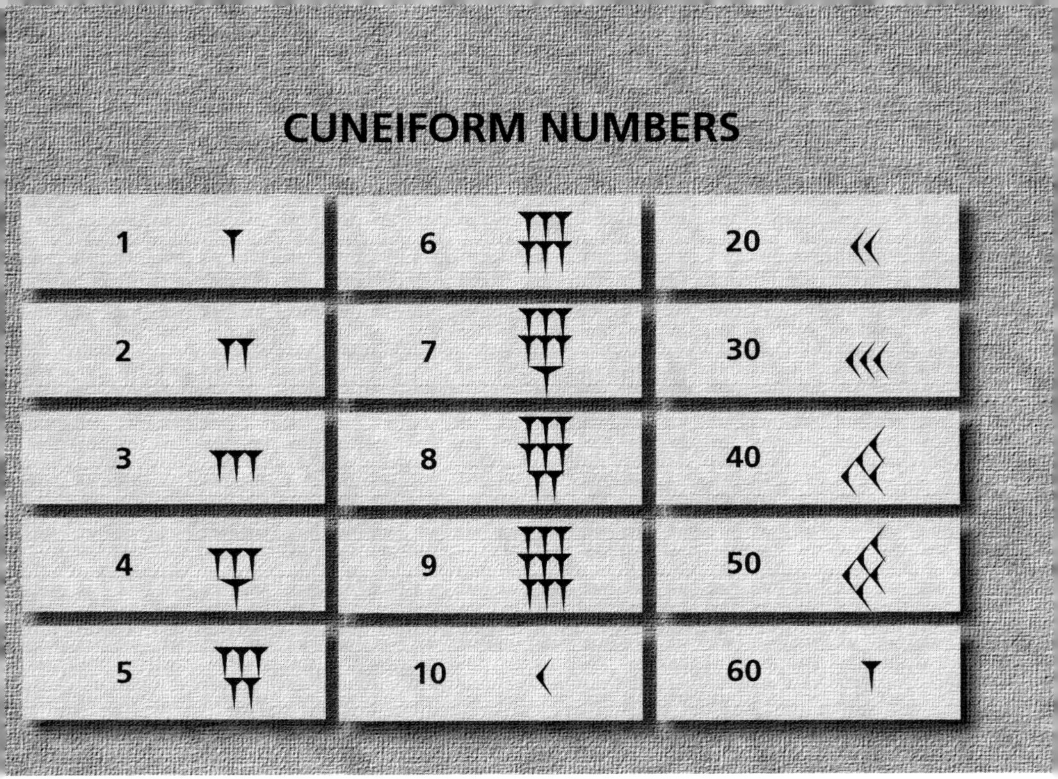

CUNEIFORM NUMBERS

1	𒁹	6	𒐚	20	𒎙
2	𒐻	7	𒐛	30	𒌍
3	𒐼	8	𒐜	40	𒐏
4	𒐽	9	𒐡	50	𒐐
5	𒐾	10	𒌋	60	𒁹

This illustration shows how Mesopotamians wrote numbers.

the sky. Mesopotamian astrologers developed the **zodiac**. The zodiac is an imaginary circle in the sky. It is divided into 12 parts. Each part has its own name and **constellation**. A constellation is a series of stars that form a shape.

COMMON CUNEIFORM SYMBOLS

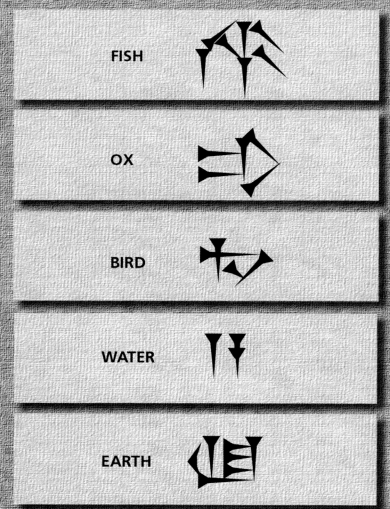

FISH

OX

BIRD

WATER

EARTH

This illustration shows common cuneiform symbols and what they mean.

How Do We Know?

Archaeologists learn about Mesopotamian people by reading **cuneiform** tablets. Figuring out how to read cuneiform was not easy. The Mesopotamian people spoke many different languages. Some tablets were written in more than one language. Scholars who knew one language used their knowledge to figure out the others.

An American named Samuel Noah Kramer (1897-1990) became an expert in Sumer language and culture. He wrote books to share his knowledge with the world. Without his studies, the world would have known much less about the Sumerians.

Mesopotamian Sites

Besides cuneiform, archaeologists study **artifacts** to discover how Mesopotamians lived. An artifact is an object that was made or used by people in the past.

The ruins of famous city-states contain many artifacts. Sir Leonard Woolley was a famous archaeologist. He uncovered many graves at Ur in the 1920s and 1930s. The graves contained jewelry, headdresses, statues, and musical instruments.

There are many Mesopotamian treasures still hidden underground. In 1989, archaeologists found gold jewelry in a grave at Nimrud. One necklace had 28 pendants, or hanging ornaments. They also found 72 pairs of earrings, bowls and cups made of gold, and vases made of bronze.

Mesopotamia in the Modern World

Some people remember the culture of Mesopotamia by recreating its architecture. Parts of the Ishtar Gate have been rebuilt.

▲ This is a reconstruction of Babylon's Ishtar Gate, which is in modern Iran.

People had to pass through the Ishtar Gate to enter **ancient** Babylon.

Mesopotamia still affects how people live today. Cars would not be possible if Mesopotamians had not invented the wheel. Our system of time is based on the Mesopotamian system of counting. Even some of our stories and laws are based on Mesopotamian culture.

Glossary

ancient (AYN-shunt)—very old

archaeologist (ar-kee-OL-uh-jist)—a scientist who studies the past

architecture (AR-ki-tek-chur)—the style and way a building is made

artifact (ART-uh-fakt)—an object that was made or used by humans in the past

bitumen (bit-OH-min)—a natural tar used to cement bricks or make boats waterproof

chariot (CHA-ree-uht)—a wheeled vehicle where the rider stands and is pulled by an animal

constellation (kon-stuh-LAY-shuhn)—a group of stars that form a shape

culture (KUHL-chur)—the way of life, ideas, customs, and traditions of a group of people

cuneiform (KYOO-ni-form)—a way of writing that looks like lines and wedges

empire (EM-pire)—a group of countries with one ruler

epic (EP-ik)—a long story or poem about the adventures and battles of a king, god, or hero

mosaic (moh-ZAY-ik)—a work of art created by using many small things to make a picture or pattern

pictograph (PIK-toh-graf)—a picture used as a symbol for a word or sound

pottery (POT-ur-ee)—objects made of clay, such as pots, bowls, vases, and cups

priest (PREEST)—men who served the gods and worked in temples

society (suh-SYE-uh-tee)—all the people who live in the same country or area and share the same laws and customs

stylus (STYE-luhs)—a writing tool with a thick end and a thin end

temple (TEM-puhl)—a special building used for worshiping gods

zodiac (ZOH-dee-ak)—an imaginary circle in the sky that is divided into 12 parts

Internet Sites

The Epic of Gilgamesh
http://www.hist.unt.edu/ane-09.htm

Mesopotamia in the Electronic Passport
http://www.mrdowling.com/603mesopotamia.
  html

**Minnesota State University e-Museum—
  Mesopotamia**
http://www.anthro.mankato.msus.edu/
  prehistory/middle_east/index.shtml

**The UnMuseum: Hanging Gardens of
  Babylon**
http://unmuseum.mus.pa.us/hangg.htm

Write Like A Babylonian
http://www.upennmuseum.com/cuneiform.cgi

Useful Addresses

Iraqi Interests Section—USA
1801 P Street NW
Washington, DC 20036

Museum of Archaeology and Ethnology
Department of Archaeology
Simon Fraser University
8888 University Drive
Burnaby, BC V5A 1S6
Canada

The Oriental Institute
1155 East 58th Street
Chicago, IL 60637

Index